Brandon Si[l]
Ghosts of the [

by Anne Langley
Stretton on Dunsmore, Warwickshire, England

This book is dedicated to all the children who worked at Brandon Silk Mill.

Contents

Copyright © 2001 Stretton on Dunsmore History Society.
Published by Stretton Millennium History Group.
Scanning, page make-up and design by Warwick Dipple Design, Rugby.
Printed in England by Eureka Press Ltd, Leicester.
Front cover: Mill site on the 11th Green at Brandon Wood Golf Club

Copies of this book can be obtained from local outlets or ordered from
12 Squires Road, Stretton on Dunsmore, Rugby, CV23 9HF: please enclose a cheque for £3 made out to
Stretton on Dunsmore History Society and an A5 stamped addressed envelope.

ISBN 0-9537462-1-6

Introduction

Brandon is a small village in Warwickshire, five miles east of Coventry (see sketch map below); a silk mill was shown here on nineteenth-century maps of the area. I became interested in this mill because Victorian children from my own village of Stretton on Dunsmore were working there when they should have been at school. I wanted to know when the mill was built, what it did, who worked in it and what it was like to work there. With a bit of detective work I was able to find answers to these questions, although there are still some mysteries to be solved and I have not yet found any photos of the mill.

I discovered that Brandon silk mill stood on the site of a much older water mill. The silk mill flourished for 70 years up to the end of the nineteenth century. At its peak this mill employed 170 people from surrounding villages, some of them walking eight miles a day to get there. The history of the mill illustrates many aspects of the industrial revolution. It offered useful employment to local people; but young children were working there instead of being educated, and conditions were poor with low wages and long hours in dangerous surroundings. Today Brandon Wood Golf Course stands on the mill site, and I like to imagine that the ghosts of the mill workers still linger near the 11th green. Here is the story of Brandon mill over the past 400 years.

Figure 1 Sketch map showing location of Brandon silk mill

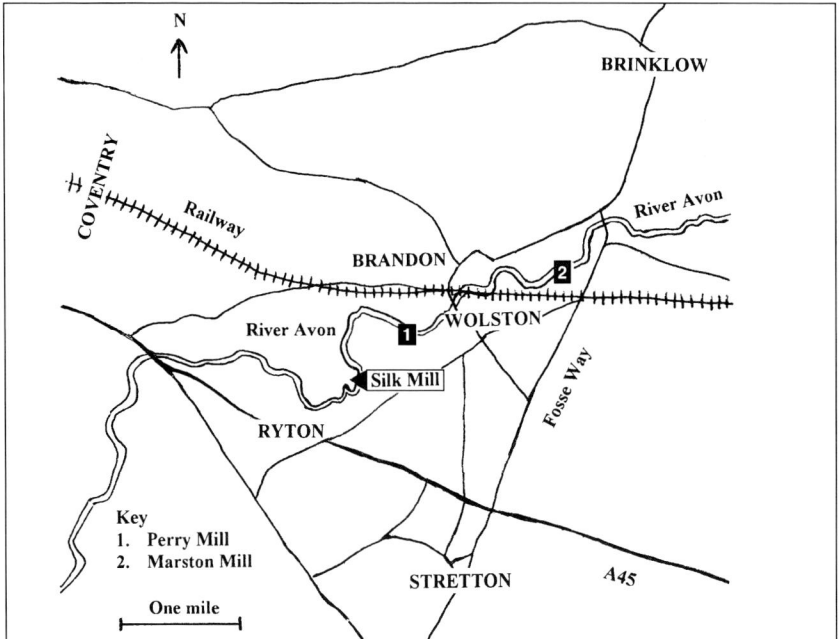

A Mill at Brandon in the Middle Ages

In 1086 the Domesday Book recorded a mill at Brandon worth 26d*. It stood on the river Avon near Brandon Castle; in the thirteenth century the castle owner gave the monks of Coombe Abbey permission to repair breaches in the mill-pond adjacent to his property. This mill was known as Perimulne or Perry mill; it ceased working early in the twentieth century, but ruins are still visible beside the Avon to the west of Wolston (1 on the map opposite). There was another mill east of Wolston, known as Marston or Mervine's mill, that still stands today though converted into a house (2 on the map opposite). Both these mills were used to grind corn from Wolston and Stretton, and a millstone from one of them is now displayed in the centre of Wolston (Figure 2 below). However neither of these Domesday mills was on the site of the silk mill, which was situated a mile south-west of the village of Brandon (see Figure 1). To avoid confusion I will call the Domesday mill at Brandon 'Perry mill', and call the silk mill 'Brandon mill' in this booklet.

*d = pennies; asterisked words (here and throughout) are explained in the Glossary on page 20

Figure 2 A local millstone in Main Street, Wolston

Mr Wilcockes' New Mill in the 17th Century

The first reference to a mill on the site of Brandon silk mill is in a map of 1630 where it was described as 'Mr Wilcockes Mill'. A little later it was described as Robert Wilcox's 'New mill' and so it was probably built in the early seventeenth century. A channel was dug about a third of a mile long, cutting off a bend in the River Avon, and a mill built straddling the millstream. Floodgates and sluices were constructed to control the flow of water. The fall of water gave sufficient power to turn a large wooden wheel like the one below. The wheel would have been connected via a drive shaft to machinery. Access to the mill was along a track from Brandon village.

Figure 3 A wooden mill wheel. This one stood at Welford-on-Avon in Warwickshire.

Fulling cloth

In 1711 the Wilcox's mill was used for fulling*: a process in the finishing of woollen cloth. After fulling, the cloth was stretched on hooks and dried by tentering (hence the expression 'to be on tenterhooks'). In the Middle Ages fulling was done by hand (or rather foot!) by tramping in a tub - rather like pressing grapes for winemaking. Indeed early fulling mills were called 'walk' mills for this reason. Then machines were invented with wooden 'feet' to flatten the cloth and later on hammers or rollers were used, driven by waterpower. During the seventeenth century there was an important woollen industry in Coventry, with fulling mills there and in the villages of Baginton and Ryton. In view of this, and the presence of two corn mills very close by, it seems likely that Mr Wilcockes' mill was originally built for fulling.

The Wilcox family of Brandon

The Wilcox family have been associated with the Brandon area for over 400 years. The family owned property in Stretton, Wolston and several other places. They did not live at the mill, nor were they millers, but landowners who lived off the rents from various properties. In 1582 Roberte Wylcox left sheep and cows, money and clothes to several members of his family. In 1674 Mr Willcox of Brandon paid tax on eight hearths so he must have been living in a substantial house. In 1711 Mary Wilcox owned the fulling mill in Brandon. In 1725 her son John married the lady of Wolston manor, Letitia Pinchin, and as a result briefly owned all three mills in the area. Later on, his widow sold the estate; she is buried in Wolston Church along with other members of the Wilcox family. A hundred years later in 1826 William Wilcox bought much of the estate again (including the two Domesday mills but not the silk mill). In the late nineteenth century the Wilcoxes lived in Wolston manor house (which used to stand behind the old iron gates next to the church). A Wilcox family hatchment* hangs on the north wall of Wolston church.
John and then Henry Wilcox were vicars of Wolston from 1872-1908. In 1875 Charles Wilcox complained that the London and North Western Railway Company was extracting too much water from the River Avon, thus affecting the workings of the Perry mill. He came to an agreement with them to pay him £10 a year for water for their locomotives and other purposes at Rugby station. In 1926 the estate passed to his daughter Mary Hoffgaard, and her son Charles took the name of Wilcox again. Mary, her father and mother, brothers and sisters are buried in Wolston churchyard (south-east of the church). Today allotment rents in Brandon are still paid to the Wilcox family, now living in South Africa.
[As you can see, the spelling of Wilcox varied over the years].

Dyeing Cloth and Making Paper in the Eighteenth Century

In 1735 Samuel Welton's will mentioned Brandon mill; he was a dyer living in Coventry, and it is possible that he used the mill at Brandon for dyeing as well as fulling cloth. Some years earlier a Mr Welton had been fined 13 shillings* by the Coventry Fullers' Guild for 'following our trade' (an early example of a demarcation dispute!). However the local fulling trade declined and by 1743 the mill was used for paper making (see box opposite). This process basically consisted of pulping rags in quantities of water to make a fibre soup, and then forming, squeezing and drying sheets of paper. The water wheel drove the hammers of the stamping machine to produce the pulp.

Improvements to the property
In the eighteenth century a fine house was added to Brandon mill, and a formal garden looking down to a reservoir was laid out. Trees were planted including a cedar and a walnut (both remain today and you can see the cedar on the front of this booklet). A handsome estate map shows the details (see the back cover of this booklet) and they are confirmed by the description of the property in the advertisement opposite. The brick footbridge across the millstream, shown on the map south of the mill, survives today (see below).

Figure 4 The footbridge over the millstream today

Advertisement in the Coventry Mercury
June 22nd 1778

TO be SOLD by AUCTION
On FRIDAY the 7th Day of August...

A large old established PAPER-MILL, consisting of
Two Vatts with the Appurtenances, together with the Tackling
Utensils, Engines, and Implements thereto belonging...also
An exceeding good New-erected MESSUAGE* or MANSION
HOUSE, with a small HOUSE thereto adjoining, with the
Mill-House, Out-Houses, Work-Houses, Warehouses, and
Drying-Houses to the said Mill belonging; and also Seventeen Acres
of Rich Pasture LAND...
the House and Mill may be Sold separate from the Land

Brandon Silk Mill – Errors and additions to note

Page 5 John Wilcox was not the son of Mary Wilcox, and he married
Letitia Pinchin in 1700 (not 1725).
The allotments mentioned are in Wolston (not Brandon).

Page 7 In the 1750s the paper mill belonged to Thomas Ashby and later
to his son-in-law Walter Lacon (both papermakers). Walter went
bankrupt in 1778 (hence the auction described). The original map
(on the back cover) was made for another auction of Brandon mill
in 1792. The mill was sold in 1797 to John Wilson who rented it to
George Herbert in 1828; his heirs sold it to George in 1848.

Page 19 Apologies to Tony Kenney (not Kelly) for mis-spelling his name.

Brandon Silk Mill in the Nineteenth Century

Around 1826 George and William Herbert, silk throwsters* in Coventry, acquired Brandon mill and converted it into a silk mill. This silk-throwing mill was first mentioned in a trade directory of 1828/9. In a throwing* mill raw silk (spun by silk worms) was turned into threads suitable for weaving. A series of activities was involved, the most important being winding* and doubling to produce stronger threads. After throwing the silk would have been passed to a dyer and then a weaver to make the finished product.

The history of silk throwing
Originally silk was wound by hand; then semi-industrial methods were used whereby young boys were required to run to and fro in sheds for up to 15 miles a day. The first machines to be introduced were simple wooden devices, initially operated by hand and later by water power. Thomas Lombe visited Italy as an industrial spy and brought back the expertise to set up a throwing mill in Derby in 1717 (alleged to have been the first textile factory in Britain). Most throwing was carried out in the Midlands and further machines (some adapted from cotton spinning) were invented to mechanise the process. Steam power was introduced during the nineteenth century.

Figure 5 A Victorian bonnet trimmed and tied with ribbons

The Coventry silk industry
Coventry was a traditional centre of the silk industry, famous for its ribbon weaving, and so most of the silk thread produced at Brandon would have ended up as colourful ribbons trimming ladies' dresses, bonnets and hair. There was a long tradition of hand weaving locally, involving whole families of men, women and children. Mechanisation was initially resisted and in 1831 there was a riot in Coventry when machines were smashed and the factory owner badly beaten. However steam-powered looms were gradually introduced and by 1851 half the working population of Coventry was involved in the silk industry. The removal of duties on imported silk goods in 1860 had a devastating effect as cheap foreign imports flooded in. Some manufacturers survived

by becoming more efficient and diversifying, but there was widespread unemployment leading to poverty and emigration of silk-weavers. All the local silk-throwing mills closed including Brandon mill, which was sold in 1867 (see below) and used for farming and brewing for a couple of years. However in 1869 it was bought by Tom Iliffe, a silk broker from Coventry who restored the silk-throwing business. It thrived for 30 more years as the only local silk-throwing mill, but closed around 1898 as artificial silk began to appear and the natural-silk industry declined further. (See Appendix 2).

Brandon silk-throwing mill was auctioned in 1867 and described as follows:

PARTICULARS

The Mill is three stories, 76 feet by 22 feet, with Warehouses, Winding Room, 90 feet long; Stove, Washhouse, and other Offices underneath, Engine House, Chimney Stack, &c.

The Driving Machinery consists of a capital 16-feet iron overshot* Water Wheel, a superior twelve-horse power high pressure Steam Engine, by Hill, in excellent working order; fifteen-horse Tubular Boiler, Shafting and Driving Wheel, and iron steam heating pipes throughout.

The RESIDENCE, which has been recently enlarged and improved, affords every accommodation for a family, with good Servants' Offices, Lawn and Garden, newly-built three-stall Stable, and Loose Box, with Loft over, and Coach Houses, Cart Sheds, Piggeries, and other Outbuildings.

Also SIX brick-built and slated COTTAGES, in good repair. The MEADOW LAND is rich. There is an ancient eel trap on the River, which is a source of considerable profit, the River abounding with fish...

The valuable MACHINERY consisting of Throwing mills, 1,678 Spindles, Spinning Mills, 800 Spindles, Doubling Frames, 266 Spindles, Cleaning Frames, 904 Spindles, Winding Engines, 704 Spindles, with Warehouse Fixtures, Lathe and Smiths' Tools...

The MILLS are available for Flour or Paper Mills, or for a Brewery, or any purpose requiring an abundant supply of water. The property is sold with the annual tenancy of the Carriage Road into Wolston Lane, at a Rent of £10, which Road is in addition to the Road belonging to the Property over the Estate of JAMES BEECH Esq., into Brandon Lane.

The inventory below includes delightful details suggesting that a farmer lived in the mill house and the mill was used for brewing cider and beer at that time.

1869 Brandon Mill House Inventory [extracts]
Bill of sale Mr Henry Harvey Turner

New Milch Cow

Bay Half bred Gelding

Single Bridle, Hunting saddle

2 Knife Chaff Machine

Hen & 9 eggs - Laying boxes

¹/₂ Box of Artificial [manure]

Pantry

Zinc Bucket & Stool

6 Milk tins, 2 Cream ditto

Patent Weighing Machine

Larder

8 pieces dinner service

Quantity of wine bottles

12 Table K and forks

Kitchen

Zinc bucket and Coal scuttle

Piece of bacon about 14 lbs

Store room

Mangold & Swede seed

Cattle powders & drenches

Dining room

6 Cane seated chairs

table, sofa, fender

Breakfast room

Pair of straw palliasses

Flock bed, Bolster, 2 sheets

Bedrooms [3 used as such]

No. 4, 21 sacks

Workshop

Quantity of sawn Crab Tree
    for Mill use

Brewhouse

Lead Pipes from Soft Water
    Pump to Copper

Bells, carriages & fittings

Warehouse

Bean Mill, Malt Mill and
    dressing mill; Cider mill

In Mill

Machines, 2 Pairs of [Mill] Stones

The Ghosts 'Speak'

The child labourer in 1851
I'm Hannah Clarke, ten years old, and working at Brandon mill as a silk winder. I live in a cottage on Poor's Plott in Stretton on Dunsmore. Father's a bricklayer and mother's a washerwoman. My sister Fanny's thirteen and she works at the mill too. We walk across the fields to the factory and back two miles each way. It's all right going, but coming back up the hill I get very tired. It's not so bad in the summer when we look for birds' nests and pick berries, but I hate it in winter when we're coming home in the dark. I've got two younger sisters who don't work yet; they help mother round the house.

The 'Engine driver' in 1871
I'm Thomas Edginton and I live in Brandon Mill cottages. I look after the steam engine at the mill. I come from Coventry but my wife, Rebecca, was born in Tewkesbury where the owner's family used to have a silk-throwing business. My daughter Sarah's eleven and she works as a silk winder; Thomas who's nine goes to school and the four youngest are at home. We've a lodger, eighteen-year-old Sarah from Tewkesbury, who works at the mill.

The mill owner in 1861
I am Edmund Septimus Ratliff, aged 32, silk throwster and owner of Brandon silk mill where I employ 28 men, 30 women, 54 girls and 30 boys. I live in the mill house with my wife Mary and six children: five boys and a girl. The two oldest boys go to school. We have four servants living in: a cook, a housemaid, a nurse and a kitchen maid. The gardener and the groom live in Mill Row cottages close by, along with several of the mill workers.

The unmarried mother in 1881
I'm Roseanne Newman, nineteen years old. My mother died when I was little leaving seven of us orphans. Ten years ago we lived in Ryton and me and my sister and brothers worked in the silk mill. Unfortunately I got pregnant last year and had a baby in the Rugby workhouse*. Father's forgiven me now and I live with him and baby Anna in Bourton; he's an agricultural labourer.

[Post-script: Roseanne worked as a servant, had another illegitimate baby and died in 1884, aged 24. The second baby, called Rose, was baptised the following year. Her younger sister also had an illegitimate baby in 1884.]

The mill worker in 1881

I'm Ishmael Kenning, silk throwster, and I live at No. 2 Brandon Mill Cottages. It's a terraced house with an outdoor lavatory shared with my neighbours. Five of us work at the silk mill: my wife Mary, my son William who's eighteen and my daughters Emma and Eliza who're fifteen and sixteen. We've six younger children too so there are eleven of us living in two rooms. It's a tight squeeze, but we manage by sleeping the children at both ends of the bed. I'd like to move to a bigger place, but this is handy for work, and Mary can come back at lunchtime to look to the children.

[The stories above are based on censuses and parish records]

Figure 6   1905 map of the site showing mill buildings and workers' cottages

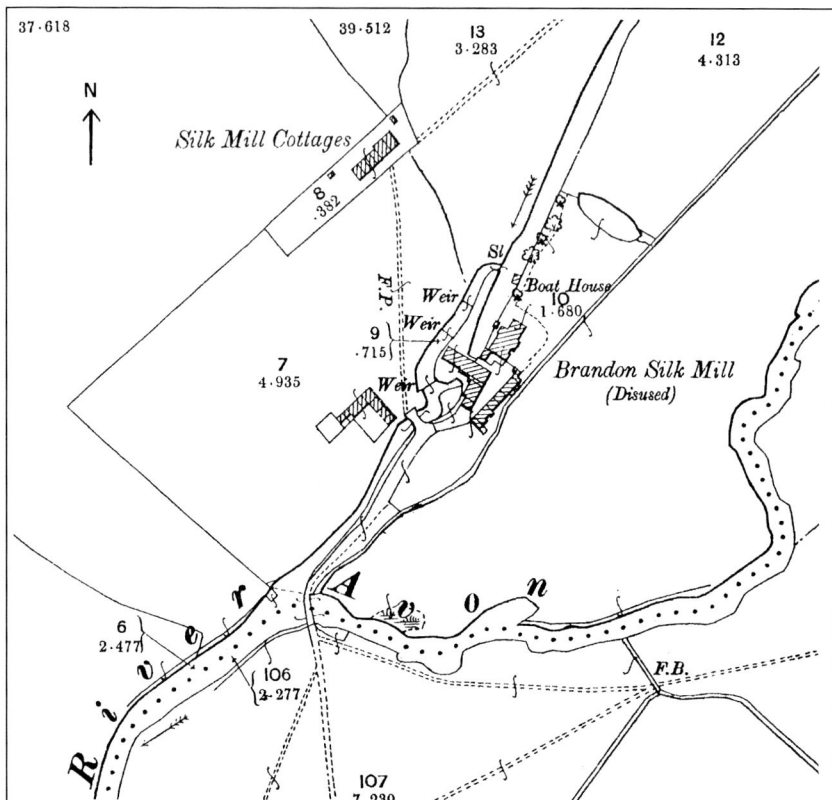

Child Labour in Nineteenth-century Britain

Very young children worked in Britain during the nineteenth century, often in appalling conditions. Successive Acts of Parliament restricted hours of work and abolished employment of very young children. Silk mills were initially exempt since they relied on child labour, but the 1844 Factory Act abolished employment of children under eight and full-time employment of children under 13 in all textile mills, and required part-timers to attend school.

Figure 7   Women and children at work in a cotton-spinning mill, 1835

Conditions in a silk-throwing mill

In the 1830s Parliament published reports on the textile industry and employment of children. Throwing work was tiring, involving standing at a machine; children from the age of five were employed, the youngest needing a stool to reach the machines. Windows were kept shut to prevent silk drying out so the atmosphere was stuffy and girls sometimes fainted. There were few, unisex lavatories. In some workrooms silence was enforced to aid concentration. The conditions could lead to eyestrain or lung disease and workers sometimes cut their hands on the sharp threads. Machines were unguarded and accidents happened, with no compensation for injuries. In 1831 they worked from 6 am to 6 pm (with an hour for lunch and a break for tea). Wages were very low (5 shillings a week for a man, 3 shillings for a woman and 1-2 shillings for a child). Children were encouraged to compete for a prize (a doll for the girls and food for the boys) and then the others forced to work as hard in future. They were beaten with a strap or cane for mistakes or to keep them awake.

The Children of Stretton on Dunsmore

Stretton is a village near Brandon. In the first half of the nineteenth century some Stretton children worked on 'gimping'* (winding silk for trimmings); this was linked to the home-based, handloom weaving trade. By 1851 ten children aged 9-13 from Stretton worked at Brandon silk mill, plus a few older people. They came from poor families, many of them living in 'The Plott' – a hamlet of cottages built for labourers on the outskirts of Stretton after the enclosures. (This hamlet has now disappeared, apart from a water pump in Plott Lane.) Several of the child workers came from single parent families. Children, though badly paid, often made a vital contribution to the family finances. Children from other local villages (Brandon, Ryton on Dunsmore, Wolston and even Brinklow, four miles away) also worked at the silk mill.

The schoolmaster's tale
The Stretton schoolmaster kept a logbook from 1862 onwards. He recorded a constant struggle to persuade parents to send children to school and to prevent truancy. Children were frequently absent working, including 'the factory children' at Brandon mill. One teacher was understanding:
'The poorer classes will not deny themselves for the sake of the education of their children. Nor can they be reasonably expected to do so when 10 shillings per week is all they obtain for their labour.' (31 October 1870).
At that time rent for a cottage might have been 1-2 shillings a week. School fees were 1½ d a week and so parents who educated their child were caught in a 'double whammy': they lost the child's earnings and had to pay for schooling, which was not free until 1891. The Poor Law* authorities set a shocking example: 'compelling the children whom they relieve as paupers* to go to work at Brandon Mill as "Half Timers". One boy from this school has been forced to go and another child, 8, has been told to go. Both children are fatherless.' (11 April 1872).

The schoolmaster versus the silk mill
A night school was set up in Stretton three evenings a week for those working during the day and some factory children attended. Once half-time schooling became compulsory, factory children attended half-days and later on alternate days. As you can imagine, this disrupted the teaching of the whole school. The school attendance officer prosecuted a few parents, however the fines were small (a few shillings) and not much of a deterrent. On 26 January 1877 the schoolmaster complained to the Inspector of Factories at Coventry about the half-timers working at the silk mill, and ten children returned to the school. Shortly afterwards the mill tried to persuade him to conspire: 'Received a letter from Mr. McDonagh, Brandon Mill concerning G. F., S. B. and H. R. They are supposed to be under 11 years of age, & he wants them to be passed by as full-time workers. Placed the matter in the hands of the Factory Inspector...he sent their parents a strong letter & ordered them to send their children to school half-time.' (8 & 26 March 1877).

By 1881 primary education was compulsory (but not yet free) and in theory the battle for school attendance had been won. The census recorded just three 13 year-olds from local villages working at the silk mill, plus an 11 year-old and two 12 year-olds (working illegally). In practice, however, the school logbook recorded ongoing problems with the mill as children continued to work there throughout the 1880s and early 1890s.

Figure 8 Stretton schoolchildren and their teachers around 1900

The Owners of Brandon Silk Mill

Date	Owner	Details
1828-30	G. & W. Herbert	Brandon Mills (& Coventry) Throwsters
1835-50	George Herbert	Brandon Mill
1854	Thomas Rowbotham	Manager (George's widow was the owner)
1860-6	Edmund S. Ratliff	Silk throwster, employed 142 people in 1861
1869-88	Tom A. S. Iliffe	Employed 170, 120 female & 50 male in '71
1876	"	Employed 200 (including Brinklow mill)
1884	"	Employed 150
1891-6	William S. Cox	Silk throwster, Brandon mill

Brandon Mill Site in the Twentieth Century

The silk mill disappeared from Kelly's trade directory between 1896 and 1900 and was shown as disused on a map of 1905 (see Figure 6 on page 12). The site gradually fell into ruin and was used by Mr Corbishley who owned the adjacent Brandon Wood Farm. Some buildings became cowsheds and bricks were recycled into a grain-drying plant. There was a mulberry tree (perhaps part of an experiment in cultivating silkworms). By the 1930s there were 'a few old walls' plus traces of the old eel trap, and the bridge over the Avon had disappeared. Local children from Ryton and Wolston used to paddle and swim there at 'the old mill' in the 1940s and 50s. The site was levelled in the 1970s when Brandon Wood Golf Course was laid out.

A visit to the site of Brandon Mill
The manager of the Golf Course, Tony Smith, kindly showed me round the site of the silk mill. There are remains of a weir and sluices on the main river Avon, with walls of brick (some faced with stone) and traces of wooden gates. The millstream is still clearly visible, with water standing in it, though in a couple of places it has been filled in. The oval reservoir shown in the map on the back cover is still there, containing some water, with a cast-iron overflow pipe emerging under a tree root. Several trees from the original garden are now fine specimens: a walnut tree, a cedar tree and a pine, with box bushes in the hedgerow. The mill building itself stood where the 11th green is now, but only a small corner of brickwork survives. Part of the brick channel and sluices round the mill (marked with weirs in Figure 6 on page 12) feature on a path. A delightful brick footbridge over the millstream to the south of the mill has been preserved (see Figure 4 on page 6). One apple tree still stands in the old orchard, and bears fruit. At the south end of the millstream substantial brick foundations of the main bridge survive on both sides of the River Avon, with a metal reinforcing plate made by Watson & Huxley. The mill cottages have disappeared completely, but moles in the area turn up pieces of coal and broken bricks, slates, quarry floor tiles, pottery and glass. The pottery included a fragment of a willow-pattern plate and I like to imagine this in use on best occasions by silk workers in Victorian times.

Conclusion
Looking at the site today it is hard to believe that a busy mill stood here for three centuries, and that hundreds of people worked in this peaceful country setting: fulling cloth, making paper, and throwing silk. I hope you enjoyed finding out about the mill and those who worked there as much as I have. And maybe one day you will see the ghost of a mill worker on the 11th green!

Appendix 1

Mr Iliffe's Silk Mill at Brinklow

In 1872 Mr Iliffe expanded his business by opening a second silk-throwing mill in Brinklow, employing up to 50 people. However this mill only operated for about ten years. The machinery must have been driven by steam, as it stood at the south end of the main street with no river nearby. The Brinklow branch of the Oxford canal ran close by, and may have been used for transporting supplies such as coal to the mill. Children from the local school worked at this mill, and the local schoolmaster – like the master in Stretton – had irate exchanges with the manager, Mr McDonagh, who lived in Brinklow. The L-shaped mill building still stands today, though it has been substantially altered at the street end (see Figure 9 below). It was smaller than Brandon silk mill, but gives an idea of what that may have looked like.

Figure 9 The former silk-throwing mill in Broad Street, Brinklow today

Appendix 2

The Artificial Silk Factory at Wolston

At the very end of the nineteenth century Cash's set up the 'New Artificial Silk Company' in Wolston (the village next door to Brandon). Artificial silk (or rayon) was manufactured by treating wood pulp and spinning the long fibres produced. This process required good supplies of water and the factory was situated beside the river Avon. I assume that the company benefited from the skills of the former Brandon mill workers. It certainly used child labour because the Stretton schoolmaster noted children asking for certificates to go and work there in June 1900. A map of the period calls it a 'Celluloid Factory'. However it did not last long and had closed down by 1904. The site was taken over by Bluemel's cycle accessories, which later diversified into motor accessories and lasted until the 1980s. The building still stands on Wolston Business Park (see Figure 10 below) though now only partly occupied. Other artificial silk factories set up by Cash's and Courtauld's in Coventry in the early twentieth century were much more successful.

Figure 10 The former Artificial Silk Factory building in Wolston today

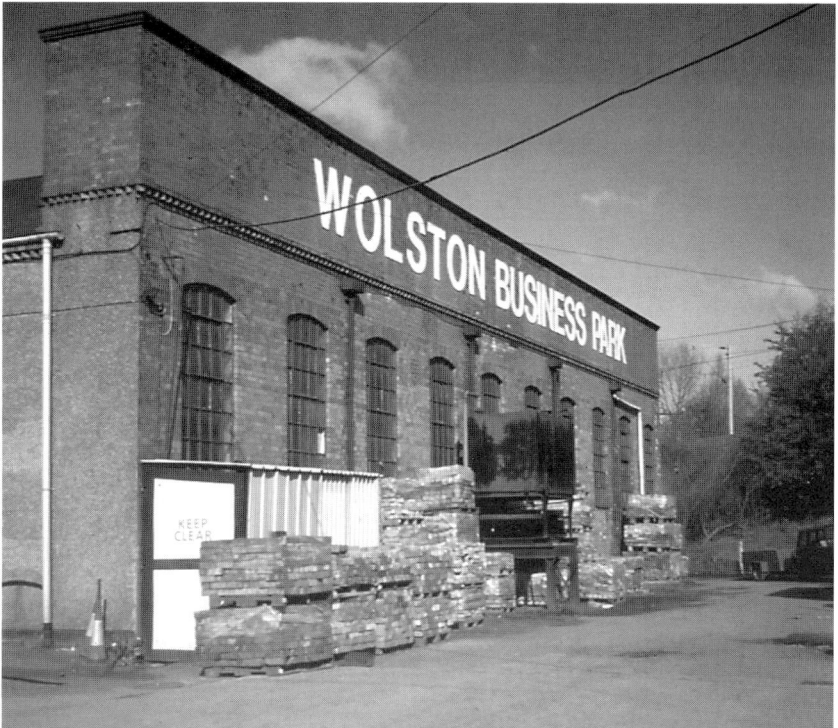

Sources, References and Acknowledgments

This booklet is based on study of a number of documents in Warwick County Record Office. The most important were:
Auction particulars (1867), CR 350/29 (see page 9).
Brandon Mill House Inventory (1869), CR 2433/31/116 (see page 10).
Censuses for villages in the area for 1851-91.
Estate map of Brandon Mill (1792), CR 350/24 (see back cover).
Index to the Wilcox family papers (not deposited).
Map of Brandon by A. Denton (1630), CR Z 203 (u).
Stretton on Dunsmore school logbooks (1862-1906), CR 699/1-3.
Trade Directories for Warwickshire.
Wolston Church records of baptisms, marriages and burials.

Other useful information came from the Coventry Local Studies Library, the Coventry Archives and the Open University Library. The following books were particularly helpful:

British Parliamentary Papers, Industrial Revolution: Children's Employment, 1831-2,
Irish University Press (1968).
British Parliamentary Papers, Industrial Revolution: Textiles, 1831-2,
Irish University Press (1968).
Brynca's Low: A History of the village of Brinklow,
D. Lindsay, Brinklow History Group (1995).
History of Technology,
eds C. Singer et al, Oxford University Press (1958).
Stretton on Dunsmore: the making of a Warwickshire Village,
Stretton Millennium History Group (2000).
The Silk Industry of the UK,
F. Warner, Dranes (1922).
Victoria County History for Warwickshire,
ed. R. Pugh, Oxford University Press (1969).
Women and Industrialisation,
J. Lown, Polity Press (1990).

I am very grateful to Richard Chamberlaine-Brothers and other archivists at the Warwick County Record Office for valuable help with research and for permission to quote extracts from the Stretton School Logbooks and to reproduce the map on the back cover. *Figure 3* comes from *Rambles by Rivers* by J. Thorne (1845) page 183. The following also kindly gave permission for reproduction of material: *Figure 6,* Ordnance Survey © Crown Copyright NC/01/385; *Figure 7,* Mary Evans Picture Library; *Figure 8,* Stretton Millennium History Group. I produced *Figures 1, 2, 4, 5, 9 and 10.*
Tony Smith, manager of Brandon Wood Golf Course, gave me access to the mill site and generously shared his expertise with me as did several others: Mr S. Atkins, Mr P. Grantham, Ray and Victor Healey, Tony Kelly, Richard Postlethwaite, Caroline Wetton and Alan Woodley. My husband Peter gave encouragement throughout and both he and my daughter Rosemary made helpful editorial comments.

Glossary

Fulling   A finishing process in the production of cloth that degreases cloth and makes it heavier and more compact by shrinking and beating. Fulling required quantities of water and soap or fuller's earth.

Gimping   Winding silk for making trimmings.

Hatchment   A diamond-shaped tablet with the coat of arms of a dead person.

Messuage   A house together with the outbuildings and land belonging to it.

Overshot water wheel   A wheel driven by water that flows into compartments at the top of the wheel, the weight of water turning the wheel as it falls.

Pauper   A poor person receiving assistance from the Poor Law Authorities.

Penny   Pre-decimal coin worth 0.4p (written 1d).

Poor Law   A basic system of welfare to provide for the poor in each district.

Shilling   Pre-decimal coin worth 5p (written 1s or 1/-).

Throwing   Treating raw silk to prepare it for dyeing and weaving. The heart of the process consisted of twisting and doubling the silk filaments to make threads strong enough for weaving into cloth, ribbons etc. Thus silk throwing was the equivalent of spinning for other textiles such as cotton.

Throwster   One who throws silk. The term was used for the mill owner and the factory hands. It was also used as an adjective eg a 'throwstering mill'.

Winding   Winding silk threads from large reels onto bobbins prior to throwing. Initially done by hand, later by machinery.

Workhouse   Basic accommodation provided by the Poor Law authorities for the destitute poor: chiefly orphans, the unemployed and the aged.